HOME

HOME
Celebrating Autumn & Winter

John Grady Burns

By

Jill Helmer   John Grady Burns   Kathy Stewart

Photography by
Bartram Nason

Collaborators Publishing
Atlanta, Georgia

HOME
Celebrating Autumn & Winter

For information or to order copies contact
Evergreenbook@gmail.com or visit
https://www.evergreendecorators.com.

Published by
Collaborators Publishing 2017

Edited by
Jill Helmer and Bookhouse Group, Inc.

Photographed by
Bartram Nason
http://www.bartramnason.com.

Additional photographs
pp. 31, 33, 59, 80, 81 by Micah Bible
p. 70 by Jill Helmer

Creative Design by
Laurie Moffitt of Compōz Design LLC
laurie@compoz.com

Printed in the USA

ISBN: 978-1-5323-3921-9

First Printing 2017

Celebrating home

John Grady Burns, Kathy Stewart, and Jill Helmer, the co-authors and collaborators of design and publishing, pause while on a photo shoot in the Blue Ridge Mountains.

giving *thanks*

I n 2009 we released our first book, *Evergreen—Decorating With Colours of the Season*. We had hoped to inspire people with their holiday decorating, to possibly help them simplify the decorating task, and to encourage them to entertain more and share the warmth they created in their own homes.

As *Evergreen* went into numerous reprints, individuals would repeatedly tell us they refer to their tattered copies every Christmas. We realized we had indeed met our goal. That alone fed our own enthusiasm and spirit as the holidays approached each year.

We have been equally fortunate with the success of our second book *Collections—Sharing the Passion*. Appealing to a broad audience of collectors, decorators, and coffee table book lovers, we find people as amazed at the different types and displays of collections as we were and still are.

Producing both books was hard work—physically and mentally exhausting, but at the same time we had fun. If we had not, *Home—Celebrating Autumn & Winter* would never have been published. During the process we learned a lot about the people who allowed us to photograph in their homes, a lot about ourselves, and a lot about each other. We are grateful to these people and to other individuals who contributed in making *Home* become a reality.

Adelaide and Dal, Alvin and Don, Angela and Hunt, Betsy and Larry, Billie, Claire and George, Daisy and John, Elizabeth, Julie and Don, Katherine and Rich, Linda and Buster, Liz, Margaret and Ike, Micah, Nancy and Coleman, Patty and Gordon, Priscilla and Linton, Sandra and Rusty, and the owners and managers of privately owned locations. We would also like to thank an incredible team of designers we work with every Christmas holiday season transforming a massive space into a festive one. Their works are featured throughout the Winter section. A special thanks to our talented friend Rebecca who went beyond just friendship in making pinecone, magnolia, and fir garlands and wreaths that graced the homes on many of the pages in *Home—Celebrating Autumn & Winter*. We are grateful to our friends, Mary and Eric, for giving us use of their home, Hilltop, when photographing in the mountains of North Carolina.

We would be remiss if we did not thank our patient photographer Bartram Nason and art director Laurie Moffitt. Without their patience and talent *Home* would not be. A thank you also to Rob Levin and his guidance, and of course our partners who have remained supportive and encouraging. ◆

contents

INTRODUCTION

Autumn—cooler days and nights, apples and pumpkins and gourds galore, and an amazing spectrum of color everywhere one looks. These are the images we all have once the calendar flips over to September. To quote F. Scott Fitzgerald: "Life starts all over again when it gets crisp in the fall."

Regardless of where one resides, September brings changes. School starts, businesses begin to buckle down again, and those lazy days of summer come to an abrupt halt. With summer behind us we begin to look forward to autumn and all the wonderful things it brings. In parts of the South, the thermometer hardly takes notice while those in other areas of the country are bundled up in sweaters and hoping an early snowfall is not far behind. No matter the temperature or what part of the country, leaves begin to fall like giant snowflakes. The ground is covered in acorns and nuts and spiders are hurriedly spinning their webs. Apple, pumpkin, and pecan pies are being made and suddenly Thanksgiving has arrived. This is a time when family and friends gather.

Winter—shorter days and longer nights, deciduous trees with their sculptural shapes, and evergreens displaying a colorful spectrum of greens are part of the next several months. As soon as the Thanksgiving holiday is behind us we scurry around preparing for the next holiday. Soon a new year is upon us and we are wondering where the past year went. The winter season with its months of cold is beginning to settle in. Some will take comfort just being in the warmth of a roaring fire, or curled up reading a good book, or settling in for a winter's nap while in the background Vivaldi's *Winter* plays. Winter can be a tranquil and peaceful time—if we allow it. ◆

—Jill Helmer, John Grady Burns, Kathy Stewart

AUTUMN
a season of reflection

The sky is different, the sun is different, and a calm seems to happen with that first hint of autumn. Certain smells bring back memories and we find ourselves reflecting on hayrides, Halloween, Thanksgiving, and then thoughts of autumn coming to an end. Watching and listening to children dream up their costumes brings on a flood of Halloween memories from our childhood. Our mothers or some other talented person constructed our simple homemade outfits. These costumes were usually limited to witches, ghosts, princesses, and monsters, but to us they were the greatest. As we headed out into the night, jack-o'-lanterns lit the way. ◆

Natural harvest

Pumpkins and the woody vine of bittersweet are perfectly suited in this outdoor setting. Both will weather the elements throughout the season.

FALL

I'm so glad I live in a world where there are Octobers.
—L.M. Montgomery, *Anne of Green Gables*

Green carpet

An eye-catching carpet of lush green moss is the perfect setting for these bright orange pumpkins.

Rustic beauty

This old zinc sink makes a great prep area. Here, it holds foliage and flowers waiting to be brought inside and arranged.

An apple a day

There are enough apples here for a full day of baking. They make a clever centerpiece when teamed with the iron geese from the garden.

Nothing says fall more than pumpkins and crisp autumn colors that dance throughout the home.

Inviting entries

Entrances make wonderful settings for pumpkins and gourds. There is no reason to limit decorating to just one or two pumpkins. Grouping pumpkins can make a huge impact and send the message that autumn has arrived with a welcome! Making the investment in a lot of pumpkins will be rewarding for the long display time throughout autumn.

Unpredictable pairings

White pumpkins and an assortment of other colors have come into vogue the last decade. They lend themselves well in decorating as shown here paired with the white barnacle-covered driftwood.

Solitude in the country

Enchanting evenings

Before the annual Halloween pumpkin float on this pond, ghost maidens have been known to make their presence in the woods.

"*How beautifully leaves grow old. How full of light and color are their last days.*"
—John Burroughs

Welcome home

Walking a shaded trail with crispy leaves beneath your feet, a pet that frolics on a cool afternoon hike, or a porch that welcomes you home—this is autumn.

Delightfully fresh

A roadside market with local pumpkins, gourds, ciders, barbeque, homemade breads, jellies, and cakes makes for a fun shopping experience.

Gourmet gatherings

Whether for personal enjoyment, family or for the pleasure of guests, adding decoration to the kitchen is always enjoyed.

"*Autumn is a second spring when every leaf is a flower.*"
—Albert Camus

Preserving the past

During this home's construction, the columns were saved from the wrecking ball and now serve as a focal point from the living room.

Brighten the palette

A splash of bright green will add a focal point and make any room warm and inviting. Green pears and apples make great accents during the fall season.

Just a touch

The addition of bright orange in these rooms
signals autumn has arrived.

(above right) The dried arrangement is further
enhanced with the addition of a wooden basket
filled with tangerines.

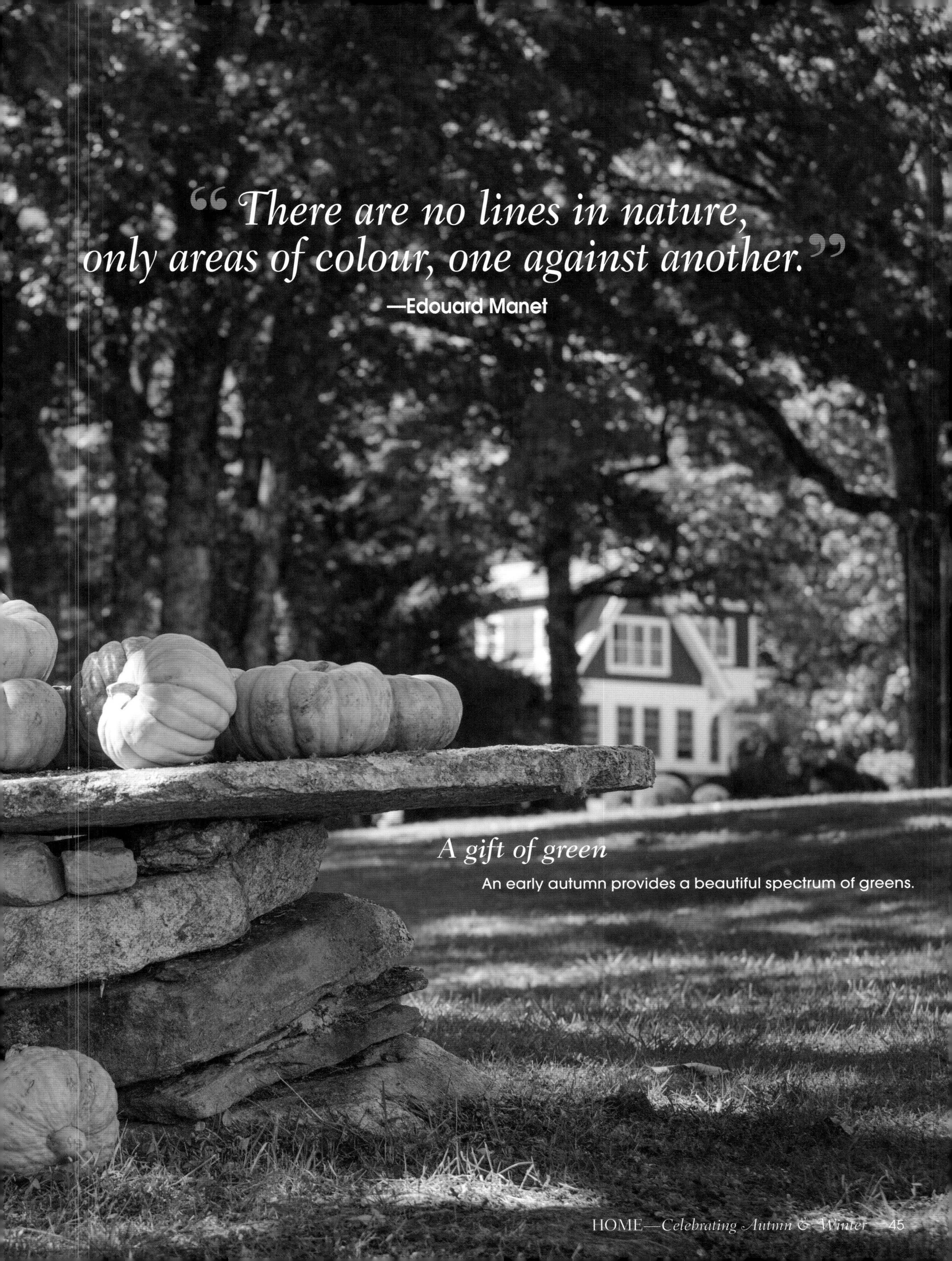

"*There are no lines in nature,*
only areas of colour, one against another."

—Edouard Manet

A gift of green

An early autumn provides a beautiful spectrum of greens.

Unexpected surprise

This window box is an unexpected surprise with its lush arrangement of bittersweet, cabbage, kale, pumpkins, heuchera, and reindeer moss.

Displaying the harvest

A collection of pumpkins is further enhanced by the addition of things from the woods—the bittersweet and moss.

At home
These pansies look at home in a naturally hollowed-out tree branch.

"The soul never thinks without a picture."
—Aristotle

It's in the details

(above) Using only lichen-covered branches with these pinecones make a striking arrangement with little effort.

> # "Study nature, love nature, stay close to nature.
> ## It will never fail you."
>
> —Frank Lloyd Wright

Nature's wonders

Just a few stems of goldenrod and crimson colored
viburnum leaves liven up this screened porch.
For the Red-headed Woodpecker (right),
it is nature's acorn that delights him.

Garden to table

Simply turning to the garden can provide decoration for almost any occasion.

Inviting

This fall tablescape is perfect on a chilly and foggy day for having friends stop in. Gathered for the season, the lichen-covered branches on the mantel will be able to stay throughout the winter.

When in doubt, use color

There is no better time than fall for working with bold colors. All of nature is a spectrum of vivid colors. Learn to work with nature and the rest will fall into place with your decor.

"*Orange is the happiest color.*"

—Frank Sinatra

When choosing a pumpkin, go for a stem with character.

Simplicity

(above) A variety of white oak acorns gathered early in the season makes for an interesting collection and display in this silver serving piece.

(right) Pumpkins, along with foliage and grasses gathered from the roadside, change the look of accessories on this desk as well as the feel of the room.

(left) An early September apple picked from a Nantucket garden is a simple touch that signals autumn's arrival.

The boldness of bittersweet

This mountain arbor covered with bittersweet and the garnished silver basket (left) is a reminder of nature's blazing colors.

Savoring the end of the season

A tapestry of color

Nature provides a kaleidoscope of color
from the palette of the foliage (opposite)
to the jewel tones in the turkey's feathers.

Fall to Winter

As the seasons change from autumn to winter so does decor. Here, and on the next several pages, are images of the same spaces transitioned from fall to winter. Not only do the foliage and seasonal materials change, but also the accessories.

> **"When the bold branches bid farewell to rainbow leaves—**
> **Welcome wool sweaters."**
> —B. Cybrill

Impressive transitions

This mantel decorated for autumn and
winter is as different as night and day.
Moving art from other rooms gives a fresh
look with which to work around.

WINTER
a time for comfort

The season of winter brings different thoughts to mind for everyone. For some it is looking forward to the first snowfall, or thoughts of the upcoming holidays, or a time to gather with family and friends. The short days of winter can be a time of comfort and a time of renewal. Trees have bared their souls and the abundance of berries are a feast for our feathered friends as well as a visual one for us. The smell of chimney smoke fills the air while indoors we are busying ourselves in the comfort of our homes.

Embrace the season. Afterall, it happens every year. As Robert Frost said, "You can't get too much winter in the winter." ◆

An eye on the flock

Sheep have always played a role during Christmas. This collection prominently displayed on the mantel is combined with vintage accessories making it festive and enchanting for all.

Waiting for Christmas
Don we now our gay apparel,
fa-la-la-la-la-la-la-la la!

Pretty as a Package

Decorating with art

(opposite) One can almost feel winter when
viewing these snow scenes. The bare branch in
the beautifully carved vase adds to the feel.

Anticipation

(opposite) A lot of prep work is still to be done before this Civil War home will be decked for the holidays.

(above left)) A detail of one of the Four Seasons iron chairs

(above right) A Silver Tip fir that will soon be taken inside.

Working with scale

The large sideboard in this dining room can handle
a tablescape of this scale. Cut trees will last well
into the holidays allowing the arrangement to
stay throughout the entertaining season.

The new year

This winter design can easily last through the new year holiday.

A time to gather

Turning to the yard for a variety of greenery is an easy
way to accomplish a long-lasting arrangement.

A pine sapling from the woods is a simple solution for a tabletop Christmas tree.

Ready for the holidays

The lush garland of magnolia and cedar is stunning on this secretary. Garlands and wreaths need to fit the scale of the furniture and space where they will be used.

Sharing your heritage

This old growth pecky cypress plank wall is the perfect architectural feature to showcase a collection of tartans.

Timeless

Simplicity is all it takes to make a strong statement.

Decking the hall

A collection of sterling ornaments stands out on this decorated newel post more so than had they been on the family Christmas tree.

Getting cornered

(opposite and above) Decorating only the corners of a
mantel not only makes for less work but allows any art that
may be over the mantel to remain the focal point.

Man loves company—even if it only that of a small burning candle.
—Georg C. Lichtenberg

Exquisite details

Using beautiful and luxurious ribbon will take a design to the next level. It can be as important as the design itself.

The joy of an early Christmas present

Sparkle and shine

A collection worth showcasing—
vintage tree toppers.

140

Elegant choices

Amber glass conveys a warm feeling and is a lovely
contrast to the berries and late winter camellia blossoms.

All that glitters is not necessarily gold

Using silver and platinum takes designs in a
different direction from evergreens and berries.
Both are beautiful.

A calm morning

A minimum of decoration is used to keep this
mantel looking uncluttered and restful.

What's old is new again

A charming old-fashioned tree with large colored lights
has vintage ornaments dating from the1930s and 1940s.
Next to the tree sits an antique Russian troika.

Less stress

This cottage is decorated with locally made
evergreen wreaths along with branches gathered
from the nearby woods.

Red always takes centerstage

Favorite things

(opposite) This large Pacific fir branch fills the room with a fresh fragrance and makes quite a statement in the room.

Ornaments can still be enjoyed even though a large tree is not put up for Christmas. A selection of the homeowner's favorite and most sentimental ornaments are put out for viewing.

All tied up with a ribbon and bow

Candlelight

A cold snowy day is perfect for lighting candles—
a daytime indulgence reserved for the holiday season.

164

Beautifully wrapped packages add weight and charm to this tree.

A change for winter

(above) The basket contents were changed from magazines to garlands, the white candle was substituted with red, and a different painting depicting winter were changes made for easy winter accessorizing.

(opposite) For the holiday season, the arrangement was changed, and the cones in the hollowed out tree limb were added.

Firs come in all shapes and sizes

This vintage laundry basket is perfect for displaying gifts.

A bowl of acorn ornaments is a sophisticated look in this embosssed creamware compote.

Containing beauty

An antique garden container with a tabletop tree is as beautiful as the large tree that traditionally graces this foyer.

Peppermint puffs, making a nostalgic return from the 1950's, brings a touch of merriment to the room's ambiance.

Accentuate the unusual

The Coulter pine cones take centerstage in this grouping. These cones, some of the heaviest in the world, stay on a tree for five to six years making them more difficult to come by.

66 *The perfect Christmas tree? All Christmas trees are perfect!* 99
—Charles N. Barnard

The use of only snowflakes and icicles adds elegance to this tree.

This primitive huntboard is used to display winter snow scenes paired with a simple piece of driftwood.

Mix it up

From year to year, moving decorations to different location. within the home gives a fresh new look.

> *"It's beginning to look a lot like Christmas."*
> —Meredith Wilson

Layering for the season

(above and opposite) By simply adding another layer of decoration, these winter arrangements were transformed for the Christmas holidays.

Once the crystal tree in the glass bowl (above) is removed, as well as the decor on the mirror (opposite), the remaining items could remain in place throughout the winter.

Beautiful in its simplicity

The bright green vase and red berries provide a
pop of winter color to this otherwise tranquil foyer.

Blue and green vintage ornaments were chosen to complement the turquoise vase.